The

BIBLE PROMISE BOOK

for

Fathers

BARBOUR
PUBLISHING, INC.
Uhrichsville, Ohio

Published by Barbour Publishing, Inc.
P.O. Box 719
Uhrichsville, Ohio 44683
http://www.barbourbooks.com

 Member of the
Evangelical Christian
Publishers Association

Printed in the United States of America.

The

BIBLE
PROMISE
BOOK
for

Fathers

❦

TABLE OF CONTENTS

COMFORTING

Come unto me, all ye that labour and are heavy laden, and I will give you rest.

Matthew 11:28

Yea, though I walk through the valley of the shadow of death, I will fear no evil: for thou art with me; thy rod and thy staff they comfort me.

Psalm 23:4

For the Lord himself shall descend from heaven with a shout, with the voice of the archangel, and with the trump of God: and the dead in Christ shall rise first:

Then we which are alive and remain shall be caught up together with them in the clouds, to meet the Lord in the air: and so shall we ever be with the Lord.

Wherefore comfort one another with these words.

1 Thessalonians 4:16-18

Casting all your care upon him; for he careth for you.

1 Peter 5:7

Comfort ye, comfort ye my people, saith your God.

Isaiah 40:1

Blessed are they that mourn: for they shall be comforted.

Matthew 5:4

And I will pray the Father, and he shall give you another Comforter, that he may abide with you for ever.

John 14:16

Yet man is born unto trouble, as the sparks fly upward.

I would seek unto God, and unto God would I commit my cause.

Job 5:7-8

The Spirit of the Lord GOD is upon me; because the LORD hath anointed me to preach good tidings unto the meek; he hath sent me to bind up the brokenhearted, to proclaim liberty to the captives, and the opening of the prison to them that are bound;

To proclaim the acceptable year of the LORD, and the day of vengeance of our God; to comfort all that mourn.

Isaiah 61:1-2

Blessed be God, even the Father of our Lord Jesus Christ, the Father of mercies, and the God of all comfort;

Who comforteth us in all our tribulation, that we may be able to comfort them which are in any trouble, by the comfort wherewith we ourselves are comforted of God.

For as the sufferings of Christ abound in us, so our consolation also aboundeth by Christ.

2 Corinthians 1:3-5

I will not leave you comfortless: I will come to you.

John 14:18

I remembered thy judgments of old, O LORD; and have comforted myself.

Psalm 119:52

COUNSELING

As every man hath received the gift, even so minister the same one to another, as good stewards of the manifold grace of God.

1 Peter 4:10

For unto us a child is born, unto us a son is given: and the government shall be upon his shoulder: and his name shall be called Wonderful, Counsellor, The mighty God, The everlasting Father, The Prince of Peace.

Isaiah 9:6

And all thy children shall be taught of the LORD; and great shall be the peace of thy children.

Isaiah 54:13

Now no chastening for the present seemeth to be joyous, but grievous: nevertheless afterward it yieldeth the peaceable fruit of righteousness unto them which are exercised thereby.

Hebrews 12:11

Hear counsel, and receive instruction, that thou mayest be wise in thy latter end.

Proverbs 19:20

Howbeit when he, the Spirit of truth, is come, he will guide you into all truth: for he shall not speak of himself; but whatsoever he shall hear, that shall he speak: and he will shew you things to come.

John 16:13

Give instruction to a wise man, and he will be yet wiser: teach a just man, and he will increase in learning.

Proverbs 9:9

Brethren, if a man be overtaken in a fault, ye which are spiritual, restore such an one in the spirit of meekness; considering thyself, lest thou also be tempted.

Galatians 6:1

The way of a fool is right in his own eyes: but he that hearkeneth unto counsel is wise.

Proverbs 12:15

Ointment and perfume rejoice the heart: so doth the sweetness of a man's friend by hearty counsel.

Proverbs 27:9

Where no counsel is, the people fall: but in the multitude of counsellors there is safety.

Proverbs 11:14

Without counsel purposes are disappointed: but in the multitude of counsellors they are established.

Proverbs 15:22

For whom the Lord loveth he chasteneth, and scourgeth every son whom he receiveth.

If ye endure chastening, God dealeth with you as with sons; for what son is he whom the father chasteneth not?

Hebrews 12:6-7

A wise man will hear, and will increase learning; and a man of understanding shall attain unto wise counsels.

Proverbs 1:5

COURAGEOUS

Wait on the LORD: be of good courage, and he shall strengthen thine heart: wait, I say, on the LORD.

Psalm 27:14

For God hath not given us the spirit of fear; but of power, and of love, and of a sound mind.

2 Timothy 1:7

So that we may boldly say, The Lord is my helper, and I will not fear what man shall do unto me.

Hebrews 13:6

Only let your conversation be as it becometh the gospel of Christ: that whether I come and see you, or else be absent, I may hear of your affairs, that ye stand fast in one spirit, with one mind striving together for the faith of the gospel;

And in nothing terrified by your adversaries: which is to them an evident token of perdition, but to you of salvation, and that of God.

Philippians 1:27-28

And now, little children, abide in him; that, when he shall appear, we may have confidence, and not be ashamed before him at his coming.

1 John 2:28

In the fear of the LORD is strong confidence: and his children shall have a place of refuge.

Proverbs 14:26

Watch ye, stand fast in the faith, quit you like men, be strong.

1 Corinthians 16:13

The wicked flee when no man pursueth: but the righteous are bold as a lion.

Proverbs 28:1

Having therefore, brethren, boldness to enter into the holiest by the blood of Jesus.

Hebrews 10:19

And thou, son of man, be not afraid of them, neither be afraid of their words, though briers and thorns be with thee, and thou dost dwell among scorpions: be not afraid of their words, nor be dismayed at their looks, though they be a rebellious house.

Ezekiel 2:6

Be of good courage, and he shall strengthen your heart, all ye that hope in the LORD.

Psalm 31:24

In whom we have boldness and access with confidence by the faith of him.

Ephesians 3:12

DEPENDABLE

And the Lord said, Who then is that faithful and wise steward, whom his lord shall make ruler over his household, to give them their portion of meat in due season?

Luke 12:42

And he spake a parable unto them to this end, that men ought always to pray, and not to faint.

Luke 18:1

Teach me, O LORD, the way of thy statutes; and I shall keep it unto the end.

Psalm 119:33

Be not carried about with divers and strange doctrines. For it is a good thing that the heart be established with grace; not with meats, which have not profited them that have been occupied therein.

Hebrews 13:9

And ye have forgotten the exhortation which speaketh unto you as unto children, My son, despise not thou the chastening of the Lord, nor faint when thou art rebuked of him:

Hebrews 12:5

But he that shall endure unto the end, the same shall be saved.

Matthew 24:13

Let a man so account of us, as of the ministers of Christ, and stewards of the mysteries of God.

Moreover it is required in stewards, that a man be found faithful.

1 Corinthians 4:1-2

Wherefore we labour, that, whether present or absent, we may be accepted of him.

2 Corinthians 5:9

He shall not be afraid of evil tidings: his heart is fixed, trusting in the LORD.

Psalm 112:7

Let your loins be girded about, and your lights burning;

And ye yourselves like unto men that wait for their lord, when he will return from the wedding; that when he cometh and knocketh, they may open unto him immediately.

Luke 12:35-36

For if any be a hearer of the word, and not a doer, he is like unto a man beholding his natural face in a glass:

For he beholdeth himself, and goeth his way, and straightway forgetteth what manner of man he was.

But whoso looketh into the perfect law of liberty, and continueth therein, he being not a forgetful hearer, but a doer of the work, this man shall be blessed in his deed.

James 1:23-25

My heart is fixed, O God, my heart is fixed: I will sing and give praise.

Psalm 57:7

DILIGENT

Labour not for the meat which perisheth, but for that meat which endureth unto everlasting life, which the Son of man shall give unto you: for him hath God the Father sealed.

John 6:27

Whatsoever is commanded by the God of heaven, let it be diligently done for the house of the God of heaven: for why should there be wrath against the realm of the king and his sons?

Ezra 7:23

I must work the works of him that sent me, while it is day: the night cometh, when no man can work.

John 9:4

Wherefore the rather, brethren, give diligence to make your calling and election sure: for if ye do these things, ye shall never fall:

For so an entrance shall be ministered unto you abundantly into the everlasting kingdom of our Lord and Saviour Jesus Christ.

2 Peter 1:10-11

Behold that which I have seen: it is good and comely for one to eat and to drink, and to enjoy the good of all his labour that he taketh under the sun all the days of his life, which God giveth him: for it is his portion.

Every man also to whom God hath given riches and wealth, and hath given him power to eat thereof, and to take his portion, and to rejoice in his labour; this is the gift of God.

Ecclesiastes 5:18-19

Or he that exhorteth, on exhortation: he that giveth, let him do it with simplicity; he that ruleth, with diligence; he that sheweth mercy, with cheerfulness.

Romans 12:8

The thoughts of the diligent tend only to plenteousness; but of every one that is hasty only to want.

Proverbs 21:5

Wherefore, beloved, seeing that ye look for such things, be diligent that ye may be found of him in peace, without spot, and blameless.

2 Peter 3:14

And let us not be weary in well doing: for in due season we shall reap, if we faint not.

Galatians 6:9

Therefore, my beloved brethren, be ye stedfast, unmoveable, always abounding in the work of the Lord, forasmuch as ye know that your labour is not in vain in the Lord.

1 Corinthians 15:58

Much food is in the tillage of the poor: but there is that is destroyed for want of judgment.

Proverbs 13:23

But ye, brethren, be not weary in well doing.

2 Thessalonians 3:13

DISCIPLINING

One that ruleth well his own house, having his children in subjection with all gravity;

(For if a man know not how to rule his own house, how shall he take care of the church of God?)

1 Timothy 3:4-5

Withhold not correction from the child: for if thou beatest him with the rod, he shall not die.

Thou shalt beat him with the rod, and shalt deliver his soul from hell.

Proverbs 23:13-14

He that spareth his rod hateth his son: but he that loveth him chasteneth him betimes.

Proverbs 13:24

Foolishness is bound in the heart of a child; but the rod of correction shall drive it far from him.

Proverbs 22:15

And, ye fathers, provoke not your children to wrath: but bring them up in the nurture and admonition of the Lord.

Ephesians 6:4

Correct thy son, and he shall give thee rest; yea, he shall give delight unto thy soul.

Proverbs 29:17

Now, lo, if he beget a son, that seeth all his father's sins which he hath done, and considereth, and doeth not such like,

That hath not eaten upon the mountains, neither hath lifted up his eyes to the idols of the house of Israel, hath not defiled his neighbour's wife,

Neither hath oppressed any, hath not withholden the pledge, neither hath spoiled by violence, but hath given his bread to the hungry, and hath covered the naked with a garment,

That hath taken off his hand from the poor, that hath not received usury nor increase, hath executed my judgments, hath walked in my statutes; he shall not die for the iniquity of his father, he shall surely live.

Ezekiel 18:14-17

Fathers, provoke not your children to anger, lest they be discouraged.

Colossians 3:21

Even a child is known by his doings, whether his work be pure, and whether it be right.

Proverbs 20:11

Chasten thy son while there is hope, and let not thy soul spare for his crying.

Proverbs 19:18

For God commanded, saying, Honour thy father and mother. . . .

Matthew 15:4 (partial)

Cursed be he that setteth light by his father or his mother. And all the people shall say, Amen.

Deuteronomy 27:16

DUTIFUL

Observe and hear all these words which I command thee, that it may go well with thee, and with thy children after thee for ever, when thou doest that which is good and right in the sight of the LORD thy God.

Deuteronomy 12:28

And he sought God in the days of Zechariah, who had understanding in the visions of God: and as long as he sought the LORD, God made him to prosper.

2 Chronicles 26:5

Now therefore, if ye will obey my voice indeed, and keep my covenant, then ye shall be a peculiar treasure unto me above all people: for all the earth is mine.

Exodus 19:5

And shewing mercy unto thousands of them that love me, and keep my commandments.

Exodus 20:6

And ye shall be hated of all men for my name's sake: but he that endureth to the end shall be saved.

Matthew 10:22

When a man's ways please the LORD, he maketh even his enemies to be at peace with him.

Proverbs 16:7

Save when there shall be no poor among you; for the LORD shall greatly bless thee in the land which the LORD thy God giveth thee for an inheritance to possess it:

Only if thou carefully hearken unto the voice of the LORD thy God, to observe to do all these commandments which I command thee this day.

Deuteronomy 15:4-5

Thou shalt keep therefore his statutes, and his commandments, which I command thee this day, that it may go well with thee, and with thy children after thee, and that thou mayest prolong thy days upon the earth, which the LORD thy God giveth thee, for ever.

Deuteronomy 4:40

If they obey and serve him, they shall spend their days in prosperity, and their years in pleasures.

Job 36:11

And why call ye me, Lord, Lord, and do not the things which I say?

Luke 6:46

If ye be willing and obedient, ye shall eat the good of the land.

Isaiah 1:19

See, I have set before thee this day life and good, and death and evil;

In that I command thee this day to love the LORD thy God, to walk in his ways, and to keep his commandments and his statutes and his judgments, that thou may-est live and multiply: and the LORD thy God shall bless thee in the land whither thou goest to possess it.

Deuteronomy 30:15-16

ENCOURAGING

I can do all things through Christ which strengtheneth me.

Philippians 4:13

He giveth power to the faint; and to them that have no might he increaseth strength.

Isaiah 40:29

Therefore, brethren, stand fast, and hold the traditions which ye have been taught, whether by word, or our epistle.

Now our Lord Jesus Christ himself, and God, even our Father, which hath loved us, and hath given us everlasting consolation and good hope through grace,

Comfort your hearts, and stablish you in every good word and work.

2 Thessalonians 2:15-17

And when they bring you unto the synagogues, and unto magistrates, and powers, take ye no thought how or what thing ye shall answer, or what ye shall say:

For the Holy Ghost shall teach you in the same hour what ye ought to say.

Luke 12:11-12

Bear ye one another's burdens, and so fulfil the law of Christ.

Galatians 6:2

Look not every man on his own things, but every man also on the things of others.

Philippians 2:4

Brethren, if any of you do err from the truth, and one convert him;

Let him know, that he which converteth the sinner from the error of his way shall save a soul from death, and shall hide a multitude of sins.

James 5:19-20

All scripture is given by inspiration of God, and is profitable for doctrine, for reproof, for correction, for instruction in righteousness.

2 Timothy 3:16

And whether we be afflicted, it is for your consolation and salvation, which is effectual in the enduring of the same sufferings which we also suffer: or whether we be comforted, it is for your consolation and salvation.

2 Corinthians 1:6

Ye are witnesses, and God also, how holily and justly and unblameably we behaved ourselves among you that believe:

As ye know how we exhorted and comforted and charged every one of you, as a father doth his children,

That ye would walk worthy of God, who hath called you unto his kingdom and glory.

For this cause also thank we God without ceasing, because, when ye received the word of God which ye heard of us, ye received it not as the word of men, but as it is in truth, the word of God, which effectually worketh also in you that believe.

1 Thessalonians 2:10-13

EVEN-TEMPERED

Then said Pilate unto him, Hearest thou not how many things they witness against thee?

And he answered him to never a word; insomuch that the governor marvelled greatly.

Matthew 27:13-14

Do all things without murmurings and disputings.

Philippians 2:14

He that is slow to wrath is of great understanding: but he that is hasty of spirit exalteth folly.

Proverbs 14:29

Charity suffereth long, and is kind; charity envieth not; charity vaunteth not itself, is not puffed up,

Doth not behave itself unseemly, seeketh not her own, is not easily provoked, thinketh no evil.

1 Corinthians 13:4-5

Wherefore, my beloved brethren, let every man be swift to hear, slow to speak, slow to wrath.

James 1:19

Can two walk together, except they be agreed?

Amos 3:3

A wrathful man stirreth up strife: but he that is slow to anger appeaseth strife.

Proverbs 15:18

Bless them which persecute you: bless, and curse not.

Romans 12:14

For even hereunto were ye called: because Christ also suffered for us, leaving us an example, that ye should follow his steps:
Who did no sin, neither was guile found in his mouth:
Who, when he was reviled, reviled not again; when he suffered, he threatened not; but committed himself to him that judgeth righteously.

1 Peter 2:21-23

Yet Michael the archangel, when contending with the devil he disputed about the body of Moses, durst not bring against him a railing accusation, but said, The Lord rebuke thee.

Jude 9

He that is slow to anger is better than the mighty; and he that ruleth his spirit than he that taketh a city.

Proverbs 16:32

Better is a dry morsel, and quietness therewith, than an house full of sacrifices with strife.

Proverbs 17:1

If the spirit of the ruler rise up against thee, leave not thy place; for yielding pacifieth great offences.

Ecclesiastes 10:4

He sitteth alone and keepeth silence, because he hath borne it upon him.

He putteth his mouth in the dust; if so be there may be hope.

Lamentations 3:28-29

FAITHFUL

For God so loved the world, that he gave his only begotten Son, that whosoever believeth in him should not perish, but have everlasting life.

John 3:16

Jesus said unto him, If thou canst believe, all things are possible to him that believeth.

Mark 9:23

O love the LORD, all ye his saints: for the LORD preserveth the faithful, and plentifully rewardeth the proud doer.

Psalm 31:23

It is written in the prophets, And they shall be all taught of God. Every man therefore that hath heard, and hath learned of the Father, cometh unto me.

John 6:45

For the Father himself loveth you, because ye have loved me, and have believed that I came out from God.

John 16:27

. . .ask in faith, nothing wavering. For he that wavereth is like a wave of the sea driven with the wind and tossed.

James 1:6

And he said to the woman, Thy faith hath saved thee; go in peace.

Luke 7:50

. . .be thou faithful unto death, and I will give thee a crown of life.

Revelations 2:10 (partial)

A faithful man shall abound with blessings: but he that maketh haste to be rich shall not be innocent.

Proverbs 28:20

And the Lord said, If ye had faith as a grain of mustard seed, ye might say unto this sycamine tree, Be thou plucked up by the root, and be thou planted in the sea; and it should obey you.

Luke 17:6

Whom having not seen, ye love; in whom, though now ye see him not, yet believing, ye rejoice with joy unspeakable and full of glory.

1 Peter 1:8

Who then is a faithful and wise servant, whom his lord hath made ruler over his household, to give them meat in due season?

Blessed is that servant, whom his lord when he cometh shall find so doing.

Verily I say unto you, That he shall make him ruler over all his goods.

Matthew 24:45-47

Therefore thus saith the Lord GOD, Behold, I lay in Zion for a foundation a stone, a tried stone, a precious corner stone, a sure foundation; he that believeth shall not make haste.

Isaiah 28:16

That if thou shalt confess with thy mouth the Lord Jesus, and shalt believe in thine heart that God hath raised him from the dead, thou shalt be saved.

Romans 10:9

He that believeth on the Son of God hath the witness in himself: he that believeth not God hath made him a liar; because he believeth not the record that God gave of his Son.

1 John 5:10

These things I have spoken unto you, that in me ye might have peace. In the world ye shall have tribulation: but be of good cheer; I have overcome the world.

John 16:33

As soon as Jesus heard the word that was spoken, he saith unto the ruler of the synagogue, Be not afraid, only believe.

Mark 5:36

But as many as received him, to them gave he power to become the sons of God, even to them that believe on his name:

John 1:12

He that believeth and is baptized shall be saved; but he that believeth not shall be damned.

Mark 16:16

Jesus answered and said unto them, This is the work of God, that ye believe on him whom he hath sent.

John 6:29

And blessed is he, whosoever shall not be offended in me.

Matthew 11:6

Let us draw near with a true heart in full assurance of faith, having our hearts sprinkled from an evil conscience, and our bodies washed with pure water.

Hebrews 10:22

Jesus saith unto him, Thomas, because thou hast seen me, thou hast believed: blessed are they that have not seen, and yet have believed.

John 20:29

Jesus saith unto her, Said I not unto thee, that, if thou wouldest believe, thou shouldest see the glory of God?

John 11:40

Behold, I stand at the door, and knock: if any man hear my voice, and open the door, I will come in to him, and will sup with him, and he with me.

Revelations 3:20

And Jesus answering saith unto them, Have faith in God.

For verily I say unto you, That whosoever shall say unto this mountain, Be thou removed, and be thou cast into the sea; and shall not doubt in his heart, but shall believe that those things which he saith shall come to pass; he shall have whatsoever he saith.

Mark 11:22-23

FORGIVING

But I say unto you, That ye resist not evil: but whosoever shall smite thee on thy right cheek, turn to him the other also.

And if any man will sue thee at the law, and take away thy coat, let him have thy cloak also.

And whosoever shall compel thee to go a mile, go with him twain.

Matthew 5:39-41

For if ye forgive men their trespasses, your heavenly Father will also forgive you:

But if ye forgive not men their trespasses, neither will your Father forgive your trespasses.

Matthew 6:14-15

Then came Peter to him, and said, Lord, how oft shall my brother sin against me, and I forgive him? till seven times?

Jesus saith unto him, I say not unto thee, Until seven times: but, Until seventy times seven.

Matthew 18:21-22

And when ye stand praying, forgive, if ye have ought against any: that your Father also which is in heaven may forgive you your trespasses.

But if ye do not forgive, neither will your Father which is in heaven forgive your trespasses.

Mark 11:25-26

Not rendering evil for evil, or railing for railing: but contrariwise blessing; knowing that ye are thereunto called, that ye should inherit a blessing.

1 Peter 3:9

Forbearing one another, and forgiving one another, if any man have a quarrel against any: even as Christ forgave you, so also do ye.

Colossians 3:13

The discretion of a man deferreth his anger; and it is his glory to pass over a transgression.

Proverbs 19:11

And be ye kind one to another, tender-hearted, forgiving one another, even as God for Christ's sake hath forgiven you.

Ephesians 4:32

Take heed to yourselves: If thy brother trespass against thee, rebuke him; and if he repent, forgive him.

And if he trespass against thee seven times in a day, and seven times in a day turn again to thee, saying, I repent; thou shalt forgive him.

Luke 17:3-4

If thou meet thine enemy's ox or his ass going astray, thou shalt surely bring it back to him again.

Exodus 23:4

And forgive us our sins; for we also forgive every one that is indebted to us. And lead us not into temptation; but deliver us from evil.

Luke 11:4

FRUGAL

For which of you, intending to build a tower, sitteth not down first, and counteth the cost, whether he have sufficient to finish it?

Lest haply, after he hath laid the foundation, and is not able to finish it, all that behold it begin to mock him,

Saying, This man began to build, and was not able to finish.

Luke 14:28-30

A good man leaveth an inheritance to his children's children: and the wealth of the sinner is laid up for the just.

Proverbs 13:22

There is treasure to be desired and oil in the dwelling of the wise; but a foolish man spendeth it up.

Proverbs 21:20

And he saith unto them, Whose is this image and superscription?

They say unto him, Caesar's. Then saith he unto them, Render therefore unto Caesar the things which are Caesar's; and unto God the things that are God's.

Matthew 22:20-21

A gracious woman retaineth honour: and strong men retain riches.

Proverbs 11:16

He that loveth pleasure shall be a poor man: he that loveth wine and oil shall not be rich.

Proverbs 21:17

And I say unto you, Make to yourselves friends of the mammon of unrighteousness; that, when ye fail, they may receive you into everlasting habitations.

He that is faithful in that which is least is faithful also in much: and he that is unjust in the least is unjust also in much.

If therefore ye have not been faithful in the unrighteous mammon, who will commit to your trust the true riches?

And if ye have not been faithful in that which is another man's, who shall give you that which is your own?

No servant can serve two masters: for either he will hate the one, and love the other; or else he will hold to the one, and despise the other. Ye cannot serve God and mammon.

Luke 16:9-13

Be not thou one of them that strike hands, or of them that are sureties for debts.

If thou hast nothing to pay, why should he take away thy bed from under thee?

Proverbs 22:26-27

The rich ruleth over the poor, and the borrower is servant to the lender.

Proverbs 22:7

GENEROUS

Therefore when thou doest thine alms, do not sound a trumpet before thee, as the hypocrites do in the synagogues and in the streets, that they may have glory of men. Verily I say unto you, They have their reward.

But when thou doest alms, let not thy left hand know what thy right hand doeth:

That thine alms may be in secret: and thy Father which seeth in secret himself shall reward thee openly.

Matthew 6:2-4

For the poor shall never cease out of the land: therefore I command thee, saying, Thou shalt open thine hand wide unto thy brother, to thy poor, and to thy needy, in thy land.

Deuteronomy 15:11

And if thy brother be waxen poor, and fallen in decay with thee; then thou shalt relieve him: yea, though he be a stranger, or a sojourner; that he may live with thee.

Leviticus 25:35

I have shewed you all things, how that so labouring ye ought to support the weak, and to remember the words of the Lord Jesus, how he said, It is more blessed to give than to receive.

Acts 20:35

If a brother or sister be naked, and destitute of daily food,

And one of you say unto them, Depart in peace, be ye warmed and filled; notwithstanding ye give them not those things which are needful to the body; what doth it profit?

James 2:15-16

Every man according as he purposeth in his heart, so let him give; not grudgingly, or of necessity: for God loveth a cheerful giver.

2 Corinthians 9:7

Give, and it shall be given unto you; good measure, pressed down, and shaken together, and running over, shall men give into your bosom. For with the same measure that ye mete withal it shall be measured to you again.

Luke 6:38

And he saw also a certain poor widow casting in thither two mites.

And he said, Of a truth I say unto you, that this poor widow hath cast in more than they all:

For all these have of their abundance cast in unto the offerings of God: but she of her penury hath cast in all the living that she had.

Luke 21:2-4

For ye know the grace of our Lord Jesus Christ, that, though he was rich, yet for your sakes he became poor, that ye through his poverty might be rich.

2 Corinthians 8:9

Is it not to deal thy bread to the hungry, and that thou bring the poor that are cast out to thy house? when thou seest the naked, that thou cover him; and that thou hide not thyself from thine own flesh?

Isaiah 58:7

For whosoever shall give you a cup of water to drink in my name, because ye belong to Christ, verily I say unto you, he shall not lose his reward.

Mark 9:41

He answereth and saith unto them, He that hath two coats, let him impart to him that hath none; and he that hath meat, let him do likewise.

Luke 3:11

Every man shall give as he is able, according to the blessing of the LORD thy God which he hath given thee.

Deuteronomy 16:17

If any man or woman that believeth have widows, let them relieve them, and let not the church be charged; that it may relieve them that are widows indeed.

1 Timothy 5:16

He that hath pity upon the poor lendeth unto the LORD; and that which he hath given will he pay him again.

Proverbs 19:17

Blessed is he that considereth the poor: the LORD will deliver him in time of trouble.

Psalm 41:1

Withhold not good from them to whom it is due, when it is in the power of thine hand to do it.

Say not unto thy neighbour, Go, and come again, and to morrow I will give; when thou hast it by thee.

Proverbs 3:27-28

GENTLE

Put them in mind to be subject to principalities and powers, to obey magistrates, to be ready to every good work,

To speak evil of no man, to be no brawlers, but gentle, shewing all meekness unto all men.

Titus 3:1-2

But sanctify the Lord God in your hearts: and be ready always to give an answer to every man that asketh you a reason of the hope that is in you with meekness and fear.

1 Peter 3:15

Now I Paul myself beseech you by the meekness and gentleness of Christ, who in presence am base among you, but being absent am bold toward you.

2 Corinthians 10:1

But the fruit of the Spirit is love, joy, peace, longsuffering, gentleness, goodness, faith.

Galatians 5:22

Take my yoke upon you, and learn of me; for I am meek and lowly in heart: and ye shall find rest unto your souls.

Matthew 11:29

He shall feed his flock like a shepherd: he shall gather the lambs with his arm, and carry them in his bosom, and shall gently lead those that are with young.

Isaiah 40:11

The meek will he guide in judgment: and the meek will he teach his way.

Psalm 25:9

For the LORD taketh pleasure in his people: he will beautify the meek with salvation.

Psalm 149:4

The meek shall eat and be satisfied: they shall praise the LORD that seek him: your heart shall live for ever.

Psalm 22:26

And the servant of the Lord must not strive; but be gentle unto all men, apt to teach, patient,

In meekness instructing those that oppose themselves; if God peradventure will give them repentance to the acknowledging of the truth;

And that they may recover themselves out of the snare of the devil, who are taken captive by him at his will.

2 Timothy 2:24-26

But the wisdom that is from above is first pure, then peaceable, gentle, and easy to be intreated, full of mercy and good fruits, without partiality, and without hypocrisy.

James 3:17

The LORD lifteth up the meek: he casteth the wicked down to the ground.

Psalm 147:6

But the meek shall inherit the earth; and shall delight themselves in the abundance of peace.

Psalm 37:11

GOD-FEARING

And fear not them which kill the body, but are not able to kill the soul: but rather fear him which is able to destroy both soul and body in hell.

Matthew 10:28

Moreover thou shalt provide out of all the people able men, such as fear God, men of truth, hating covetousness; and place such over them, to be rulers of thousands, and rulers of hundreds, rulers of fifties, and rulers of tens.

Exodus 18:21

Wherefore we receiving a kingdom which cannot be moved, let us have grace, whereby we may serve God acceptably with reverence and godly fear:

For our God is a consuming fire.
Hebrews 12:28-29

Saying with a loud voice, Fear God, and give glory to him; for the hour of his judgment is come: and worship him that made heaven, and earth, and the sea, and the fountains of waters.

Revelations 14:7

Fear ye not me? saith the LORD: will ye not tremble at my presence, which have placed the sand for the bound of the sea by a perpetual decree, that it cannot pass it: and though the waves thereof toss themselves, yet can they not prevail; though they roar, yet can they not pass over it?

Jeremiah 5:22

Only fear the LORD, and serve him in truth with all your heart: for consider how great things he hath done for you.

1 Samuel 12:24

The fear of the LORD is the beginning of knowledge: but fools despise wisdom and instruction.

Proverbs 1:7

O that there were such an heart in them, that they would fear me, and keep all my commandments always, that it might be well with them, and with their children for ever!

Deuteronomy 5:29

Then they that feared the LORD spake often one to another: and the LORD hearkened, and heard it, and a book of remembrance was written before him for them that feared the LORD, and that thought upon his name.

Malachi 3:16

Thou believest that there is one God; thou doest well: the devils also believe, and tremble.

James 2:19

The angel of the LORD encampeth round about them that fear him, and delivereth them.

Psalm 34:7

Having therefore these promises, dearly beloved, let us cleanse ourselves from all filthiness of the flesh and spirit, perfecting holiness in the fear of God.

2 Corinthians 7:1

Let us hear the conclusion of the whole matter: Fear God, and keep his commandments: for this is the whole duty of man.

Ecclesiastes 12:13

Wherefore, my beloved, as ye have always obeyed, not as in my presence only, but now much more in my absence, work out your own salvation with fear and trembling.

Philippians 2:12

A wise man feareth, and departeth from evil: but the fool rageth, and is confident.

Proverbs 14:16

The fear of the LORD is to hate evil: pride, and arrogancy, and the evil way, and the froward mouth, do I hate.

Proverbs 8:13

Men do therefore fear him: he respecteth not any that are wise of heart.

Job 37:24

Serve the LORD with fear, and rejoice with trembling.

Psalm 2:11

He will fulfil the desire of them that fear him: he also will hear their cry, and will save them.

Psalm 145:19

HONEST

Ye shall do no unrighteousness in judgment, in meteyard, in weight, or in measure.

Just balances, just weights, a just ephah, and a just hin, shall ye have: I am the LORD your God, which brought you out of the land of Egypt.

Leviticus 19:35-36

A false balance is abomination to the LORD: but a just weight is his delight.

Proverbs 11:1

Providing for honest things, not only in the sight of the Lord, but also in the sight of men.

2 Corinthians 8:21

Thou shalt not have in thy bag divers weights, a great and a small.

Thou shalt not have in thine house divers measures, a great and a small.

But thou shalt have a perfect and just weight, a perfect and just measure shalt thou have: that thy days may be lengthened in the land which the LORD thy God giveth thee.

For all that do such things, and all that do unrighteously, are an abomination unto the LORD thy God.

Deuteronomy 25:13-16

He that putteth not out his money to usury, nor taketh reward against the innocent. He that doeth these things shall never be moved.

Psalm 15:5

Pray for us: for we trust we have a good conscience, in all things willing to live honestly.

Hebrews 13:18

And herein do I exercise myself, to have always a conscience void of offence toward God, and toward men.

Acts 24:16

He that hath clean hands, and a pure heart; who hath not lifted up his soul unto vanity, nor sworn deceitfully.

Psalm 24:4

Thou knowest the commandments, Do not commit adultery, Do not kill, Do not steal, Do not bear false witness, Defraud not, Honour thy father and mother.

Mark 10:19

Ye shall not steal, neither deal falsely, neither lie one to another.

Leviticus 19:11

Receive us; we have wronged no man, we have corrupted no man, we have defrauded no man.

2 Corinthians 7:2

He that walketh righteously, and speaketh uprightly; he that despiseth the gain of oppressions, that shaketh his hands from holding of bribes, that stoppeth his ears from hearing of blood, and shutteth his eyes from seeing evil;

He shall dwell on high: his place of defence shall be the munitions of rocks: bread shall be given him; his waters shall be sure.

Isaiah 33:15-16

Therefore all things whatsoever ye would that men should do to you, do ye even so to them: for this is the law and the prophets.

Matthew 7:12

Then came also publicans to be baptized, and said unto him, Master, what shall we do?

And he said unto them, Exact no more than that which is appointed you.

Luke 3:12-13

Servants, obey in all things your masters according to the flesh; not with eyeservice, as menpleasers; but in singleness of heart, fearing God.

Colossians 3:22

My righteousness I hold fast, and will not let it go: my heart shall not reproach me so long as I live.

Job 27:6

And as ye would that men should do to you, do ye also to them likewise.

Luke 6:31

HOSPITABLE

Be not forgetful to entertain strangers: for thereby some have entertained angels unawares.

Hebrews 13:2

He doth execute the judgment of the fatherless and widow, and loveth the stranger, in giving him food and raiment.

Deuteronomy 10:18

Wisdom hath builded her house, she hath hewn out her seven pillars:

She hath killed her beasts; she hath mingled her wine; she hath also furnished her table.

She hath sent forth her maidens: she crieth upon the highest places of the city,

Whoso is simple, let him turn in hither: as for him that wanteth understanding, she saith to him,

Come, eat of my bread, and drink of the wine which I have mingled.

Proverbs 9:1-5

Use hospitality one to another without grudging.

1 Peter 4:9

Finally, be ye all of one mind, having compassion one of another, love as brethren, be pitiful, be courteous.

1 Peter 3:8

And if a stranger sojourn with thee in your land, ye shall not vex him.

But the stranger that dwelleth with you shall be unto you as one born among you, and thou shalt love him as thyself;. . .

Leviticus 19:33-34

Distributing to the necessity of saints; given to hospitality.

Romans 12:13

. . .be blameless, as the steward of God; not selfwilled, not soon angry, not given to wine, no striker, not given to filthy lucre;

But a lover of hospitality, a lover of good men, sober, just, holy, temperate.

Titus 1:7(partial)-8

And thou shalt not glean thy vineyard, neither shalt thou gather every grape of thy vineyard; thou shalt leave them for the poor and stranger: I am the LORD your God.

Leviticus 19:10

But when thou makest a feast, call the poor, the maimed, the lame, the blind:

And thou shalt be blessed; for they cannot recompense thee: for thou shalt be recompensed at the resurrection of the just.

Luke 14:13-14

Well reported of for good works; if she have brought up children, if she have lodged strangers, if she have washed the saints' feet, if she have relieved the afflicted, if she have diligently followed every good work.

1 Timothy 5:10

HUMBLE

The fear of the LORD is the instruction of wisdom; and before honour is humility.

Proverbs 15:33

Humble yourselves in the sight of the Lord, and he shall lift you up.

James 4:10

Hearken to me, ye that follow after righteousness, ye that seek the LORD: look unto the rock whence ye are hewn, and to the hole of the pit whence ye are digged.

Isaiah 51:1

When pride cometh, then cometh shame: but with the lowly is wisdom.

Proverbs 11:2

Whosoever therefore shall humble himself as this little child, the same is greatest in the kingdom of heaven.

Matthew 18:4

When men are cast down, then thou shalt say, There is lifting up; and he shall save the humble person.

Job 22:29

. . .Yea, all of you be subject one to another, and be clothed with humility: for God resisteth the proud, and giveth grace to the humble.

Humble yourselves therefore under the mighty hand of God, that he may exalt you in due time.

1 Peter 5:5(partial)-6

And whosoever shall exalt himself shall be abased; and he that shall humble himself shall be exalted.

Matthew 23:12

Behold even to the moon, and it shineth not; yea, the stars are not pure in his sight.

How much less man, that is a worm? and the son of man, which is a worm?

Job 25:5-6

LORD, my heart is not haughty, nor mine eyes lofty: neither do I exercise myself in great matters, or in things too high for me.

Psalm 131:1

But he giveth more grace. Wherefore he saith, God resisteth the proud, but giveth grace unto the humble.

James 4:6

Though the LORD be high, yet hath he respect unto the lowly: but the proud he knoweth afar off.

Psalm 138:6

But made himself of no reputation, and took upon him the form of a servant, and was made in the likeness of men:

And being found in fashion as a man, he humbled himself, and became obedient unto death, even the death of the cross.

Wherefore God also hath highly exalted him, and given him a name which is above every name.

Philippians 2:7-9

When he maketh inquisition for blood, he remembereth them: he forgetteth not the cry of the humble.

Psalm 9:12

Better it is to be of an humble spirit with the lowly, than to divide the spoil with the proud.

Proverbs 16:19

Surely he scorneth the scorners: but he giveth grace unto the lowly.

Proverbs 3:34

LORD, thou hast heard the desire of the humble: thou wilt prepare their heart, thou wilt cause thine ear to hear.

Psalm 10:17

For thus saith the high and lofty One that inhabiteth eternity, whose name is Holy; I dwell in the high and holy place, with him also that is of a contrite and humble spirit, to revive the spirit of the humble, and to revive the heart of the contrite ones.

Isaiah 57:15

Blessed are the poor in spirit: for theirs is the kingdom of heaven.

Matthew 5:3

By humility and the fear of the LORD are riches, and honour, and life.

Proverbs 22:4

JUST

Doth our law judge any man, before it hear him, and know what he doeth?

John 7:51

Judge not according to the appearance, but judge righteous judgment.

John 7:24

If there be a controversy between men, and they come unto judgment, that the judges may judge them; then they shall justify the righteous, and condemn the wicked.

Deuteronomy 25:1

But if ye had known what this meaneth, I will have mercy, and not sacrifice, ye would not have condemned the guiltless.

Matthew 12:7

Thou shalt not raise a false report: put not thine hand with the wicked to be an unrighteous witness.

Thou shalt not follow a multitude to do evil; neither shalt thou speak in a cause to decline after many to wrest judgment:

Neither shalt thou countenance a poor man in his cause.

Exodus 23:1-3

Thou shalt not defraud thy neighbour, neither rob him: the wages of him that is hired shall not abide with thee all night until the morning.

Thou shalt not curse the deaf, nor put a stumblingblock before the blind, but shalt fear thy God: I am the LORD.

Ye shall do no unrighteousness in judgment: thou shalt not respect the person of the poor, nor honour the person of the mighty: but in righteousness shalt thou judge thy neighbour.

Leviticus 19:13-15

To turn aside the right of a man before the face of the most High,

To subvert a man in his cause, the Lord approveth not.

Lamentations 3:35-36

How long will ye judge unjustly, and accept the persons of the wicked? Selah.

Defend the poor and fatherless: do justice to the afflicted and needy.

Deliver the poor and needy: rid them out of the hand of the wicked.

Psalm 82:2-4

And moreover I saw under the sun the place of judgment, that wickedness was there; and the place of righteousness, that iniquity was there.

I said in mine heart, God shall judge the righteous and the wicked: for there is a time there for every purpose and for every work.

Ecclesiastes 3:16-17

Many seek the ruler's favour; but every man's judgment cometh from the LORD.

Proverbs 29:26

Thus saith the LORD; Execute ye judgment and righteousness, and deliver the spoiled out of the hand of the oppressor: and do no wrong, do no violence to the stranger, the fatherless, nor the widow, neither shed innocent blood in this place.

Jeremiah 22:3

He that justifieth the wicked, and he that condemneth the just, even they both are abomination to the LORD.

Proverbs 17:15

Thou shalt not wrest the judgment of thy poor in his cause.

Keep thee far from a false matter; and the innocent and righteous slay thou not: for I will not justify the wicked.

And thou shalt take no gift: for the gift blindeth the wise, and perverteth the words of the righteous.

Exodus 23:6-8

Thus saith the LORD, Keep ye judgment, and do justice: for my salvation is near to come, and my righteousness to be revealed.

Isaiah 56:1

That no man go beyond and defraud his brother in any matter: because that the Lord is the avenger of all such, as we also have forewarned you and testified.

For God hath not called us unto uncleanness, but unto holiness.

He therefore that despiseth, despiseth not man, but God, who hath also given unto us his holy Spirit.

1 Thessalonians 4:6-8

Learn to do well; seek judgment, relieve the oppressed, judge the fatherless, plead for the widow.

Isaiah 1:17

KIND

Give to every man that asketh of thee; and of him that taketh away thy goods ask them not again.

Luke 6:30

She openeth her mouth with wisdom; and in her tongue is the law of kindness.

Proverbs 31:26

Let every one of us please his neighbour for his good to edification.

Romans 15:2

Put on therefore, as the elect of God, holy and beloved, bowels of mercies, kindness, humbleness of mind, meekness, longsuffering.

Colossians 3:12

The desire of a man is his kindness: and a poor man is better than a liar.

Proverbs 19:22

As we have therefore opportunity, let us do good unto all men, especially unto them who are of the household of faith.

Galatians 6:10

Who can have compassion on the ignorant, and on them that are out of the way; for that he himself also is compassed with infirmity.

Hebrews 5:2

Thus speaketh the LORD of hosts, saying, Execute true judgment, and shew mercy and compassions every man to his brother:

And oppress not the widow, nor the fatherless, the stranger, nor the poor; and let none of you imagine evil against his brother in your heart.

Zechariah 7:9-10

And if ye lend to them of whom ye hope to receive, what thank have ye? for sinners also lend to sinners, to receive as much again.

But love ye your enemies, and do good, and lend, hoping for nothing again; and your reward shall be great, and ye shall be the children of the Highest: for he is kind unto the unthankful and to the evil.

Luke 6:34-35

He that despiseth his neighbour sinneth: but he that hath mercy on the poor, happy is he.

Proverbs 14:21

Give to him that asketh thee, and from him that would borrow of thee turn not thou away.

Matthew 5:42

Rejoice with them that do rejoice, and weep with them that weep.

Romans 12:15

LEADING

Let no man despise thy youth; but be thou an example of the believers, in word, in conversation, in charity, in spirit, in faith, in purity.

1 Timothy 4:12

And they that have believing masters, let them not despise them, because they are brethren; but rather do them service, because they are faithful and beloved, partakers of the benefit. These things teach and exhort.

1 Timothy 6:2

Even as it is meet for me to think this of you all, because I have you in my heart; inasmuch as both in my bonds, and in the defence and confirmation of the gospel, ye all are partakers of my grace.

Philippians 1:7

Feed the flock of God which is among you, taking the oversight thereof, not by constraint, but willingly; not for filthy lucre, but of a ready mind;

Neither as being lords over God's heritage, but being ensamples to the flock.

And when the chief Shepherd shall appear, ye shall receive a crown of glory that fadeth not away.

1 Peter 5:2-4

Take heed therefore unto yourselves, and to all the flock, over the which the Holy Ghost hath made you overseers, to feed the church of God, which he hath purchased with his own blood.

Acts 20:28

Now then we are ambassadors for Christ, as though God did beseech you by us: we pray you in Christ's stead, be ye reconciled to God.

2 Corinthians 5:20

Holding fast the faithful word as he hath been taught, that he may be able by sound doctrine both to exhort and to convince the gainsayers.

Titus 1:9

But thou, O man of God, flee these things; and follow after righteousness, godliness, faith, love, patience, meekness.

Fight the good fight of faith, lay hold on eternal life, whereunto thou art also called, and hast professed a good profession before many witnesses.

I give thee charge in the sight of God, who quickeneth all things, and before Christ Jesus, who before Pontius Pilate witnessed a good confession;

That thou keep this commandment without spot, unrebukeable, until the appearing of our Lord Jesus Christ.

1 Timothy 6:11-14

Neglect not the gift that is in thee, which was given thee by prophecy. . . .

1 Timothy 4:14 (partial)

Whosoever transgresseth, and abideth not in the doctrine of Christ, hath not God. He that abideth in the doctrine of Christ, he hath both the Father and the Son.

If there come any unto you, and bring not this doctrine, receive him not into your house, neither bid him God speed:

For he that biddeth him God speed is partaker of his evil deeds.

2 John 1:9-11

A bishop then must be blameless, the husband of one wife, vigilant, sober, of good behaviour, given to hospitality, apt to teach;

Not given to wine, no striker, not greedy of filthy lucre; but patient, not a brawler, not covetous;

One that ruleth well his own house, having his children in subjection with all gravity;

(For if a man know not how to rule his own house, how shall he take care of the church of God?)

Not a novice, lest being lifted up with pride he fall into the condemnation of the devil.

Moreover he must have a good report of them which are without; lest he fall into reproach and the snare of the devil.

1 Timothy 3:2-7

Let the deacons be the husbands of one wife, ruling their children and their own houses well.

For they that have used the office of a deacon well purchase to themselves a good degree, and great boldness in the faith which is in Christ Jesus.

1 Timothy 3:12-13

LOVING (WITH GOD)

That Christ may dwell in your hearts by faith; that ye, being rooted and grounded in love,

May be able to comprehend with all saints what is the breadth, and length, and depth, and height;

And to know the love of Christ, which passeth knowledge, that ye might be filled with all the fulness of God.

Ephesians 3:17-19

He that hath my commandments, and keepeth them, he it is that loveth me: and he that loveth me shall be loved of my Father, and I will love him, and will manifest myself to him.

John 14:21

And I have declared unto them thy name, and will declare it: that the love wherewith thou hast loved me may be in them, and I in them.

John 17:26

And Jesus answered him, The first of all the commandments is, Hear, O Israel; The Lord our God is one Lord:

And thou shalt love the Lord thy God with all thy heart, and with all thy soul, and with all thy mind, and with all thy strength: this is the first commandment.

And the second is like, namely this, Thou shalt love thy neighbour as thyself. There is none other commandment greater than these.

Mark 12:29-31

Jesus said unto them, If God were your Father, ye would love me: for I proceeded forth and came from God; neither came I of myself, but he sent me.

John 8:42

The LORD hath appeared of old unto me, saying, Yea, I have loved thee with an everlasting love: therefore with lovingkindness have I drawn thee.

Jeremiah 31:3

And we know that all things work together for good to them that love God, to them who are the called according to his purpose.

Romans 8:28

I will declare thy name unto my brethren: in the midst of the congregation will I praise thee.

Psalm 22:22

Take good heed therefore unto yourselves, that ye love the LORD your God.

Joshua 23:11

Delight thyself also in the LORD; and he shall give thee the desires of thine heart.

Psalm 37:4

And we have known and believed the love that God hath to us. God is love; and he that dwelleth in love dwelleth in God, and God in him.

Herein is our love made perfect, that we may have boldness in the day of judgment: because as he is, so are we in this world.

There is no fear in love; but perfect love casteth out fear: because fear hath torment. He that feareth is not made perfect in love.

1 John 4:16-18

The LORD preserveth all them that love him. . . .

Psalm 145:20

Keep yourselves in the love of God, looking for the mercy of our Lord Jesus Christ unto eternal life.

Jude 21

And thou shalt love the LORD thy God with all thine heart, and with all thy soul, and with all thy might.

Deuteronomy 6:5

Love not the world, neither the things that are in the world. If any man love the world, the love of the Father is not in him.

1 John 2:15

My son, give me thine heart, and let thine eyes observe my ways.

Proverbs 23:26

I love them that love me; and those that seek me early shall find me.

Proverbs 8:17

As the Father hath loved me, so have I loved you: continue ye in my love.

John 15:9

MERCIFUL

Blessed are the merciful: for they shall obtain mercy.

Matthew 5:7

Therefore turn thou to thy God: keep mercy and judgment, and wait on thy God continually.

Hosea 12:6

He hath shewed thee, O man, what is good; and what doth the LORD require of thee, but to do justly, and to love mercy, and to walk humbly with thy God?

Micah 6:8

Behold, we count them happy which endure. Ye have heard of the patience of Job, and have seen the end of the Lord; that the Lord is very pitiful, and of tender mercy.

James 5:11

Blessed be the God and Father of our Lord Jesus Christ, which according to his abundant mercy hath begotten us again unto a lively hope by the resurrection of Jesus Christ from the dead.

1 Peter 1:3

For God hath concluded them all in unbelief, that he might have mercy upon all.

Romans 11:32

Mercy and truth are met together; righteousness and peace have kissed each other.

Psalm 85:10

Let not mercy and truth forsake thee: bind them about thy neck; write them upon the table of thine heart:

So shalt thou find favour and good understanding in the sight of God and man.

Proverbs 3:3-4

Be ye therefore merciful, as your Father also is merciful.

Luke 6:36

Not by works of righteousness which we have done, but according to his mercy he saved us, by the washing of regeneration, and renewing of the Holy Ghost;

Which he shed on us abundantly through Jesus Christ our Saviour;

That being justified by his grace, we should be made heirs according to the hope of eternal life.

Titus 3:5-7

For I will be merciful to their unrighteousness, and their sins and their iniquities will I remember no more.

In that he saith, A new covenant, he hath made the first old. Now that which decayeth and waxeth old is ready to vanish away.

Hebrews 8:12-13

But God, who is rich in mercy, for his great love wherewith he loved us,

Even when we were dead in sins, hath quickened us together with Christ, (by grace ye are saved.)

Ephesians 2:4-5

MODEST

But now ye rejoice in your boastings: all such rejoicing is evil.

James 4:16

Let another man praise thee, and not thine own mouth; a stranger, and not thine own lips.

Proverbs 27:2

Even so the tongue is a little member, and boasteth great things. Behold, how great a matter a little fire kindleth!

James 3:5

Be not rash with thy mouth, and let not thine heart be hasty to utter any thing before God: for God is in heaven, and thou upon earth: therefore let thy words be few.

Ecclesiastes 5:2

Let no man deceive himself. If any man among you seemeth to be wise in this world, let him become a fool, that he may be wise.

1 Corinthians 3:18

A man's pride shall bring him low: but honour shall uphold the humble in spirit.

Proverbs 29:23

If I must needs glory, I will glory of the things which concern mine infirmities.

2 Corinthians 11:30

Thus saith the LORD, Let not the wise man glory in his wisdom, neither let the mighty man glory in his might, let not the rich man glory in his riches:

Jeremiah 9:23

Boast not thyself of to morrow; for thou knowest not what a day may bring forth.

Proverbs 27:1

Shall the axe boast itself against him that heweth therewith? or shall the saw magnify itself against him that shaketh it? as if the rod should shake itself against them that lift it up, or as if the staff should lift up itself, as if it were no wood.

Isaiah 10:15

Whoso boasteth himself of a false gift is like clouds and wind without rain.

Proverbs 25:14

. . .Be not wise in your own conceits.

Romans 12:16 (partial)

Before destruction the heart of man is haughty, and before honour is humility.

Proverbs 18:12

And base things of the world, and things which are despised, hath God chosen, yea, and things which are not, to bring to nought things that are:

That no flesh should glory in his presence.

1 Corinthians 1:28-29

PATIENT

For whatsoever things were written aforetime were written for our learning, that we through patience and comfort of the scriptures might have hope.

Now the God of patience and consolation grant you to be likeminded one toward another according to Christ Jesus.

Romans 15:4-5

Here is the patience of the saints: here are they that keep the commandments of God, and the faith of Jesus.

Revelations 14:12

Rest in the LORD, and wait patiently for him: fret not thyself because of him who prospereth in his way, because of the man who bringeth wicked devices to pass.

Cease from anger, and forsake wrath: fret not thyself in any wise to do evil.

For evildoers shall be cut off: but those that wait upon the LORD, they shall inherit the earth.

Psalm 37:7-9

For ye have need of patience, that, after ye have done the will of God, ye might receive the promise.

Hebrews 10:36

And so, after he had patiently endured, he obtained the promise.

Hebrews 6:15

Be patient therefore, brethren, unto the coming of the Lord. Behold, the husbandman waiteth for the precious fruit of the earth, and hath long patience for it, until he receive the early and latter rain.

Be ye also patient; stablish your hearts: for the coming of the Lord draweth nigh.

James 5:7-8

Knowing this, that the trying of your faith worketh patience.

But let patience have her perfect work, that ye may be perfect and entire, wanting nothing.

James 1:3-4

And not only so, but we glory in tribulations also: knowing that tribulation worketh patience;

And patience, experience; and experience, hope.

Romans 5:3-4

But in all things approving ourselves as the ministers of God, in much patience, in afflictions, in necessities, in distresses.

2 Corinthians 6:4

Now we exhort you, brethren, warn them that are unruly, comfort the feebleminded, support the weak, be patient toward all men.

1 Thessalonians 5:14

That ye be not slothful, but followers of them who through faith and patience inherit the promises.

Hebrews 6:12

In your patience possess ye your souls.

Luke 21:19

But that on the good ground are they, which in an honest and good heart, having heard the word, keep it, and bring forth fruit with patience.

Luke 8:15

And the Lord direct your hearts into the love of God, and into the patient waiting for Christ.

2 Thessalonians 3:5

Wherefore seeing we also are compassed about with so great a cloud of witnesses, let us lay aside every weight, and the sin which doth so easily beset us, and let us run with patience the race that is set before us.

Hebrews 12:1

Better is the end of a thing than the beginning thereof: and the patient in spirit is better than the proud in spirit.

Be not hasty in thy spirit to be angry: for anger resteth in the bosom of fools.

Ecclesiastes 7:8-9

For what glory is it, if, when ye be buffeted
for your faults, ye shall take it patiently?
but if, when ye do well, and suffer for it, ye
take it patiently, this is acceptable with
God.

1 Peter 2:20

To them who by patient continuance in
well doing seek for glory and honour and
immortality, eternal life.

Romans 2:7

PEACEFUL

And to esteem them very highly in love for
their work's sake. And be at peace among
yourselves.

1 Thessalonians 5:13

Blessed are the peacemakers: for they
shall be called the children of God.

Matthew 5:9

Deceit is in the heart of them that imagine
evil: but to the counsellors of peace is joy.

Proverbs 12:20

And the fruit of righteousness is sown in
peace of them that make peace.

James 3:18

Endeavouring to keep the unity of the
Spirit in the bond of peace.

Ephesians 4:3

Flee also youthful lusts: but follow righteousness, faith, charity, peace, with them
that call on the Lord out of a pure heart.

2 Timothy 2:22

Glory to God in the highest, and on earth
peace, good will toward men.

Luke 2:14

For he that will love life, and see good
days, let him refrain his tongue from evil,
and his lips that they speak no guile:
Let him eschew evil, and do good; let
him seek peace, and ensue it.

1 Peter 3:10-11

And he shall judge among the nations, and
shall rebuke many people: and they shall
beat their swords into plowshares, and
their spears into pruninghooks: nation
shall not lift up sword against nation, neither shall they learn war any more.

Isaiah 2:4

I exhort therefore, that, first of all, suppli-
cations, prayers, intercessions, and giving
of thanks, be made for all men;
For kings, and for all that are in
authority; that we may lead a quiet and
peaceable life in all godliness and honesty.

1 Timothy 2:1-2

Follow peace with all men, and holiness,
without which no man shall see the Lord.

Hebrews 12:14

Behold, how good and how pleasant it is
for brethren to dwell together in unity!
Psalm 133:1

If it be possible, as much as lieth in you,
live peaceably with all men.
Romans 12:18

PERSEVERING

Let us hold fast the profession of our faith
without wavering; (for he is faithful that
promised.)
Hebrews 10:23

That the trial of your faith, being much
more precious than of gold that perisheth,
though it be tried with fire, might be found
unto praise and honour and glory at the
appearing of Jesus Christ.
1 Peter 1:7

Stand fast therefore in the liberty wherewith Christ hath made us free, and be not
entangled again with the yoke of bondage.
Galatians 5:1

But the path of the just is as the shining
light, that shineth more and more unto the
perfect day.
Proverbs 4:18

Praying always with all prayer and supplication in the Spirit, and watching thereunto with all perseverance and supplication for all saints.

Ephesians 6:18

Then said Jesus to those Jews which believed on him, If ye continue in my word, then are ye my disciples indeed.

John 8:31

To him that overcometh will I grant to sit with me in my throne, even as I also overcame, and am set down with my Father in his throne.

Revelations 3:21

Ye therefore, beloved, seeing ye know these things before, beware lest ye also, being led away with the error of the wicked, fall from your own stedfastness.

2 Peter 3:17

Confirming the souls of the disciples, and exhorting them to continue in the faith, and that we must through much tribulation enter into the kingdom of God.

Acts 14:22

Who shall separate us from the love of Christ? shall tribulation, or distress, or persecution, or famine, or nakedness, or peril, or sword?

Romans 8:35

Wherefore take unto you the whole armour of God, that ye may be able to withstand in the evil day, and having done all, to stand.

Ephesians 6:13

For now we live, if ye stand fast in the Lord.

1 Thessalonians 3:8

Therefore, my brethren dearly beloved and longed for, my joy and crown, so stand fast in the Lord, my dearly beloved.

Philippians 4:1

For the which cause I also suffer these things: nevertheless I am not ashamed: for I know whom I have believed, and am persuaded that he is able to keep that which I have committed unto him against that day.

Hold fast the form of sound words, which thou hast heard of me, in faith and love which is in Christ Jesus.

2 Timothy 1:12-13

For we are made partakers of Christ, if we hold the beginning of our confidence stedfast unto the end.

Hebrews 3:14

Though he fall, he shall not be utterly cast down: for the LORD upholdeth him with his hand.

Psalm 37:24

Thou therefore endure hardness, as a good soldier of Jesus Christ.

2 Timothy 2:3

He that hath an ear, let him hear what the Spirit saith unto the churches; He that overcometh shall not be hurt of the second death.

Revelations 2:11

For I am persuaded, that neither death, nor life, nor angels, nor principalities, nor powers, nor things present, nor things to come,

Nor height, nor depth, nor any other creature, shall be able to separate us from the love of God, which is in Christ Jesus our Lord.

Romans 8:38-39

POWERFUL (MIGHTY)

But ye shall receive power, after that the Holy Ghost is come upon you: and ye shall be witnesses unto me both in Jerusalem, and in all Judaea, and in Samaria, and unto the uttermost part of the earth.

Acts 1:8

And they were astonished at his doctrine: for his word was with power.

Luke 4:32

Finally, my brethren, be strong in the Lord, and in the power of his might.

Ephesians 6:10

O God, thou art terrible out of thy holy places: the God of Israel is he that giveth strength and power unto his people. Blessed be God.

Psalm 68:35

Both riches and honour come of thee, and thou reignest over all; and in thine hand is power and might; and in thine hand it is to make great, and to give strength unto all.

1 Chronicles 29:12

By pureness, by knowledge, by longsuffering, by kindness, by the Holy Ghost, by love unfeigned,

By the word of truth, by the power of God, by the armour of righteousness on the right hand and on the left.

2 Corinthians 6:6-7

And he said unto me, My grace is sufficient for thee: for my strength is made perfect in weakness. Most gladly therefore will I rather glory in my infirmities, that the power of Christ may rest upon me.

2 Corinthians 12:9

That your faith should not stand in the wisdom of men, but in the power of God.

1 Corinthians 2:5

The righteous also shall hold on his way, and he that hath clean hands shall be stronger and stronger.

Job 17:9

But they that wait upon the LORD shall renew their strength; they shall mount up with wings as eagles; they shall run, and not be weary; and they shall walk, and not faint.

Isaiah 40:31

That ye might walk worthy of the Lord unto all pleasing, being fruitful in every good work, and increasing in the knowledge of God;

Strengthened with all might, according to his glorious power, unto all patience and longsuffering with joyfulness.

Colossians 1:10-11

Be not thou therefore ashamed of the testimony of our Lord, nor of me his prisoner: but be thou partaker of the afflictions of the gospel according to the power of God.

2 Timothy 1:8

For the kingdom of God is not in word, but in power.

1 Corinthians 4:20

Now unto him that is able to do exceeding abundantly above all that we ask or think, according to the power that worketh in us.

Ephesians 3:20

And what is the exceeding greatness of his power to us-ward who believe, according to the working of his mighty power,

Which he wrought in Christ, when he raised him from the dead, and set him at his own right hand in the heavenly places.

Ephesians 1:19-20

And have tasted the good word of God, and the powers of the world to come.

Hebrews 6:5

For though he was crucified through weakness, yet he liveth by the power of God. For we also are weak in him, but we shall live with him by the power of God toward you.

2 Corinthians 13:4

Seek the LORD and his strength, seek his face continually.

1 Chronicles 16:11

For our gospel came not unto you in word only, but also in power, and in the Holy Ghost, and in much assurance; as ye know what manner of men we were among you for your sake.

1 Thessalonians 1:5

PRAYERFUL

Pray without ceasing.

1 Thessalonians 5:17

Rejoicing in hope; patient in tribulation; continuing instant in prayer.

Romans 12:12

And shall not God avenge his own elect, which cry day and night unto him, though he bear long with them?

Luke 18:7

But thou, when thou prayest, enter into thy closet, and when thou hast shut thy door, pray to thy Father which is in secret; and thy Father which seeth in secret shall reward thee openly.

But when ye pray, use not vain repetitions, as the heathen do: for they think that they shall be heard for their much speaking.

Matthew 6:6-7

Give ear to my words, O LORD, consider my meditation.

Hearken unto the voice of my cry, my King, and my God: for unto thee will I pray.

My voice shalt thou hear in the morning, O LORD; in the morning will I direct my prayer unto thee, and will look up.

Psalm 5:1-3

The LORD is nigh unto all them that call upon him, to all that call upon him in truth.

Psalm 145:18

But we will give ourselves continually to prayer, and to the ministry of the word.

Acts 6:4

Praying always with all prayer and supplication in the Spirit, and watching thereunto with all perseverance and supplication for all saints.

Ephesians 6:18

I waited patiently for the LORD; and he inclined unto me, and heard my cry.

Psalm 40:1

If my people, which are called by my name, shall humble themselves, and pray, and seek my face, and turn from their wicked ways; then will I hear from heaven, and will forgive their sin, and will heal their land.

2 Chronicles 7:14

Confess your faults one to another, and pray one for another, that ye may be healed. The effectual fervent prayer of a righteous man availeth much.

James 5:16

Likewise the Spirit also helpeth our infirmities: for we know not what we should pray for as we ought: but the Spirit itself maketh intercession for us with groanings which cannot be uttered.

Romans 8:26

The sacrifice of the wicked is an abomination to the LORD: but the prayer of the upright is his delight.

Proverbs 15:8

. . .I will pray with the spirit, and I will pray with the understanding also: I will sing with the spirit, and I will sing with the understanding also.

1 Corinthians 14:15 (partial)

Ask, and it shall be given you; seek, and ye shall find; knock, and it shall be opened unto you:

For every one that asketh receiveth; and he that seeketh findeth; and to him that knocketh it shall be opened.

Matthew 7:7-8

Because he hath inclined his ear unto me, therefore will I call upon him as long as I live.

Psalm 116:2

I will therefore that men pray every where, lifting up holy hands, without wrath and doubting.

1 Timothy 2:8

Yet the LORD will command his lovingkindness in the daytime, and in the night his song shall be with me, and my prayer unto the God of my life.

Psalm 42:8

Oh that men would praise the LORD for his goodness, and for his wonderful works to the children of men!

Psalm 107:15

So that they cause the cry of the poor to come unto him, and he heareth the cry of the afflicted.

Job 34:28

PROTECTING

Be thou my strong habitation, whereunto I may continually resort: thou hast given commandment to save me; for thou art my rock and my fortress.

Psalm 71:3

Thou hast also given me the shield of thy salvation: and thy right hand hath holden me up, and thy gentleness hath made me great.

Psalm 18:35

Above all, taking the shield of faith, wherewith ye shall be able to quench all the fiery darts of the wicked.

Ephesians 6:16

The LORD is good, a strong hold in the day of trouble; and he knoweth them that trust in him.

Nahum 1:7

The LORD is my rock, and my fortress, and my deliverer; my God, my strength, in whom I will trust; my buckler, and the horn of my salvation, and my high tower.

Psalm 18:2

The LORD liveth; and blessed be my rock; and exalted be the God of the rock of my salvation.

2 Samuel 22:47

Our soul waiteth for the LORD: he is our help and our shield.

Psalm 33:20

The name of the LORD is a strong tower: the righteous runneth into it, and is safe.

Proverbs 18:10

For thou art my rock and my fortress; therefore for thy name's sake lead me, and guide me.

Psalm 31:3

For thou, LORD, wilt bless the righteous; with favour wilt thou compass him as with a shield.

Psalm 5:12

He shall cover thee with his feathers, and under his wings shalt thou trust: his truth shall be thy shield and buckler.

Psalm 91:4

And he said, The LORD is my rock, and my fortress, and my deliverer;

The God of my rock; in him will I trust: he is my shield, and the horn of my salvation, my high tower, and my refuge, my saviour; thou savest me from violence.

2 Samuel 22:2-3

Cast thy burden upon the LORD, and he shall sustain thee: he shall never suffer the righteous to be moved.

Psalm 55:22

Every word of God is pure: he is a shield unto them that put their trust in him.

Proverbs 30:5

PROVIDING

But if any provide not for his own, and specially for those of his own house, he hath denied the faith, and is worse than an infidel.

1 Timothy 5:8

He becometh poor that dealeth with a slack hand: but the hand of the diligent maketh rich.

Proverbs 10:4

For even when we were with you, this we commanded you, that if any would not work, neither should he eat.

2 Thessalonians 3:10

Not slothful in business; fervent in spirit; serving the Lord.

Romans 12:11

The hand of the diligent shall bear rule: but the slothful shall be under tribute.

Proverbs 12:24

Whatsoever thy hand findeth to do, do it with thy might; for there is no work, nor device, nor knowledge, nor wisdom, in the grave, whither thou goest.

Ecclesiastes 9:10

Wealth gotten by vanity shall be diminished: but he that gathereth by labour shall increase.

Proverbs 13:11

He that tilleth his land shall be satisfied with bread: but he that followeth vain persons is void of understanding.

Proverbs 12:11

I know that there is no good in them, but for a man to rejoice, and to do good in his life.

And also that every man should eat and drink, and enjoy the good of all his labour, it is the gift of God.

Ecclesiastes 3:12-13

Love not sleep, lest thou come to poverty; open thine eyes, and thou shalt be satisfied with bread.

Proverbs 20:13

Let him that stole steal no more: but rather let him labour, working with his hands the thing which is good, that he may have to give to him that needeth.

Ephesians 4:28

The spider taketh hold with her hands, and is in kings' palaces.

Proverbs 30:28

And that ye study to be quiet, and to do your own business, and to work with your own hands, as we commanded you;

That ye may walk honestly toward them that are without, and that ye may have lack of nothing.

1 Thessalonians 4:11-12

The soul of the sluggard desireth, and hath nothing: but the soul of the diligent shall be made fat.

Proverbs 13:4

PRUDENT

I wisdom dwell with prudence, and find out knowledge of witty inventions.

Proverbs 8:12

For the ear trieth words, as the mouth tasteth meat.

Let us choose to us judgment: let us know among ourselves what is good.

Job 34:3-4

Even as I please all men in all things, not seeking mine own profit, but the profit of many, that they may be saved.

1 Corinthians 10:33

A good man sheweth favour, and lendeth: he will guide his affairs with discretion.

Psalm 112:5

He that handleth a matter wisely shall find good: and whoso trusteth in the LORD, happy is he.

The wise in heart shall be called prudent: and the sweetness of the lips increaseth learning.

Proverbs 16:20-21

He that troubleth his own house shall inherit the wind: and the fool shall be servant to the wise of heart.

Proverbs 11:29

Who is wise, and he shall understand these things? prudent, and he shall know them? for the ways of the LORD are right, and the just shall walk in them: but the transgressors shall fall therein.

Hosea 14:9

Agree with thine adversary quickly, whiles thou art in the way with him; lest at any time the adversary deliver thee to the judge, and the judge deliver thee to the officer, and thou be cast into prison.

Matthew 5:25

A prudent man concealeth knowledge: but the heart of fools proclaimeth foolishness.

Proverbs 12:23

The simple believeth every word: but the prudent man looketh well to his going.

Proverbs 14:15

All things are lawful unto me, but all things are not expedient: all things are lawful for me, but I will not be brought under the power of any.

1 Corinthians 6:12

A prudent man foreseeth the evil, and hideth himself: but the simple pass on, and are punished.

Proverbs 22:3

I said, I will take heed to my ways, that I sin not with my tongue: I will keep my mouth with a bridle, while the wicked is before me.

Psalm 39:1

REPENTANT

He looketh upon men, and if any say, I have sinned, and perverted that which was right, and it profited me not;

He will deliver his soul from going into the pit, and his life shall see the light.

Job 33:27-28

Likewise, I say unto you, there is joy in the presence of the angels of God over one sinner that repenteth.

Luke 15:10

Repent ye therefore, and be converted, that your sins may be blotted out, when the times of refreshing shall come from the presence of the Lord.

Acts 3:19

. . .I will have mercy, and not sacrifice: for I am not come to call the righteous, but sinners to repentance.

Matthew 9:13 (partial)

He that covereth his sins shall not prosper: but whoso confesseth and forsaketh them shall have mercy.

Proverbs 28:13

Repent therefore of this thy wickedness, and pray God, if perhaps the thought of thine heart may be forgiven thee.

Acts 8:22

And the times of this ignorance God winked at; but now commandeth all men every where to repent.

Acts 17:30

Draw nigh to God, and he will draw nigh to you. Cleanse your hands, ye sinners; and purify your hearts, ye double minded.

James 4:8

And saying, The time is fulfilled, and the kingdom of God is at hand: repent ye, and believe the gospel.

Mark 1:15

Remember therefore how thou hast received and heard, and hold fast, and repent. If therefore thou shalt not watch, I will come on thee as a thief, and thou shalt not know what hour I will come upon thee.

Revelations 3:3

Or despisest thou the riches of his goodness and forbearance and longsuffering; not knowing that the goodness of God leadeth thee to repentance?

Romans 2:4

Seek ye the LORD while he may be found, call ye upon him while he is near:

Let the wicked forsake his way, and the unrighteous man his thoughts: and let him return unto the LORD, and he will have mercy upon him; and to our God, for he will abundantly pardon.

Isaiah 55:6-7

. . .turn unto the LORD your God: for he is gracious and merciful, slow to anger, and of great kindness, and repenteth him of the evil.

Joel 2:13 (partial)

REPUTABLE

A good name is better than precious ointment; and the day of death than the day of one's birth.

Ecclesiastes 7:1

A good name is rather to be chosen than great riches, and loving favour rather than silver and gold.

Proverbs 22:1

Every man's work shall be made manifest: for the day shall declare it, because it shall be revealed by fire; and the fire shall try every man's work of what sort it is.

1 Corinthians 3:13

And they shall call them, The holy people, The redeemed of the LORD: and thou shalt be called, Sought out, A city not forsaken.

Isaiah 62:12

Ye also, as lively stones, are built up a spiritual house, an holy priesthood, to offer up spiritual sacrifices, acceptable to God by Jesus Christ.

1 Peter 2:5

But he that doeth truth cometh to the light, that his deeds may be made manifest, that they are wrought in God.

John 3:21

Neither do men light a candle, and put it under a bushel, but on a candlestick; and it giveth light unto all that are in the house.

Let your light so shine before men, that they may see your good works, and glorify your Father which is in heaven.

Matthew 5:15-16

Ye shall know them by their fruits. Do men gather grapes of thorns, or figs of thistles?

Even so every good tree bringeth forth good fruit; but a corrupt tree bringeth forth evil fruit.

A good tree cannot bring forth evil fruit, neither can a corrupt tree bring forth good fruit.

Every tree that bringeth not forth good fruit is hewn down, and cast into the fire.

Wherefore by their fruits ye shall know them.

Matthew 7:16-20

Therefore seeing we have this ministry, as we have received mercy, we faint not;

But have renounced the hidden things of dishonesty, not walking in craftiness, nor handling the word of God deceitfully; but by manifestation of the truth commending ourselves to every man's conscience in the sight of God.

2 Corinthians 4:1-2

———— ∞ ————

Now therefore ye are no more strangers
and foreigners, but fellow citizens with the
saints, and of the household of God;

And are built upon the foundation of
the apostles and prophets, Jesus Christ
himself being the chief corner stone.

Ephesians 2:19-20

Blessed is the man that walketh not in the
counsel of the ungodly, nor standeth in the
way of sinners, nor sitteth in the seat of the
scornful.

Psalm 1:1

RESPONSIBLE

Now he that planteth and he that watereth
are one: and every man shall receive his
own reward according to his own labour.

1 Corinthians 3:8

The soul that sinneth, it shall die. The son
shall not bear the iniquity of the father,
neither shall the father bear the iniquity of
the son: the righteousness of the righteous
shall be upon him, and the wickedness of
the wicked shall be upon him.

Ezekiel 18:20

And they were both righteous before God,
walking in all the commandments and
ordinances of the Lord blameless.

Luke 1:6

For by thy words thou shalt be justified, and by thy words thou shalt be condemned.

Matthew 12:37

. . .I am he which searcheth the reins and hearts: and I will give unto every one of you according to your works.

Revelations 2:23 (partial)

Dearly beloved, I beseech you as strangers and pilgrims, abstain from fleshly lusts, which war against the soul;

Having your conversation honest among the Gentiles: that, whereas they speak against you as evildoers, they may by your good works, which they shall behold, glorify God in the day of visitation.

Submit yourselves to every ordinance of man for the Lord's sake: whether it be to the king, as supreme;

Or unto governors, as unto them that are sent by him for the punishment of evildoers, and for the praise of them that do well.

For so is the will of God, that with well doing ye may put to silence the ignorance of foolish men:

As free, and not using your liberty for a cloke of maliciousness, but as the servants of God.

1 Peter 2:11-16

For every man shall bear his own burden.

Galatians 6:5

And he said, Now also let it be according
unto your words: he with whom it is found
shall be my servant; and ye shall be blameless.

Genesis 44:10

Therefore I will judge you, O house of
Israel, every one according to his ways,
saith the Lord GOD. Repent, and turn yourselves from all your transgressions; so
iniquity shall not be your ruin.

Ezekiel 18:30

That ye may be blameless and harmless,
the sons of God, without rebuke, in the
midst of a crooked and perverse nation,
among whom ye shine as lights in the
world.

Philippians 2:15

RIGHTEOUS

Whereby are given unto us exceeding
great and precious promises: that by these
ye might be partakers of the divine nature,
having escaped the corruption that is in
the world through lust.

2 Peter 1:4

Then shall the righteous shine forth as the sun in the kingdom of their Father. Who hath ears to hear, let him hear.

Matthew 13:43

LORD, who shall abide in thy tabernacle? who shall dwell in thy holy hill?

He that walketh uprightly, and worketh righteousness, and speaketh the truth in his heart.

Psalm 15:1-2

But if thou shalt indeed obey his voice, and do all that I speak; then I will be an enemy unto thine enemies, and an adversary unto thine adversaries.

Exodus 23:22

If we confess our sins, he is faithful and just to forgive us our sins, and to cleanse us from all unrighteousness.

1 John 1:9

The righteous cry, and the LORD heareth, and delivereth them out of all their troubles.

Psalm 34:17

And it shall come to pass, if thou shalt hearken diligently unto the voice of the LORD thy God, to observe and to do all his commandments which I command thee this day, that the LORD thy God will set thee on high above all nations of the earth.

Deuteronomy 28:1

The LORD will not suffer the soul of the righteous to famish: but he casteth away the substance of the wicked.

Proverbs 10:3

Ye that love the LORD, hate evil: he preserveth the souls of his saints; he delivereth them out of the hand of the wicked.
Light is sown for the righteous. . . .

Psalm 97:10-11 (partial)

Blessed are they which are persecuted for righteousness' sake: for theirs is the kingdom of heaven.

Matthew 5:10

He withdraweth not his eyes from the righteous: but with kings are they on the throne; yea, he doth establish them for ever, and they are exalted.

Job 36:7

Then shall thy light break forth as the morning, and thine health shall spring forth speedily: and thy righteousness shall go before thee; the glory of the LORD shall be thy rereward.

Isaiah 58:8

A righteous man hateth lying: but a wicked man is loathsome, and cometh to shame.

Proverbs 13:5

Then shall he answer them, saying, Verily I say unto you, Inasmuch as ye did it not to one of the least of these, ye did it not to me.

And these shall go away into everlasting punishment: but the righteous into life eternal.

Matthew 25:45-46

But know that the LORD hath set apart him that is godly for himself: the LORD will hear when I call unto him.

Psalm 4:3

He that followeth after righteousness and mercy findeth life, righteousness, and honour.

Proverbs 21:21

The eyes of the LORD are upon the righteous, and his ears are open unto their cry.

Psalm 34:15

The righteous shall be glad in the LORD, and shall trust in him; and all the upright in heart shall glory.

Psalm 64:10

Blessed are they which do hunger and thirst after righteousness: for they shall be filled.

Matthew 5:6

Know ye not that the unrighteous shall not inherit the kingdom of God? Be not deceived. . . .

1 Corinthians 6:9 (partial)

SELF-CONTROL

And every man that striveth for the mastery is temperate in all things. Now they do it to obtain a corruptible crown; but we an incorruptible.

1 Corinthians 9:25

Hast thou found honey? eat so much as is sufficient for thee, lest thou be filled therewith, and vomit it.

Proverbs 25:16

Let your moderation be known unto all men. The Lord is at hand.

Philippians 4:5

For if ye live after the flesh, ye shall die: but if ye through the Spirit do mortify the deeds of the body, ye shall live.

Romans 8:13

And beside this, giving all diligence, add to your faith virtue; and to virtue knowledge;

And to knowledge temperance; and to temperance patience; and to patience godliness;

2 Peter 1:5-6

. . .be sober, grave, temperate, sound in faith, in charity, in patience.

Titus 2:2 (partial)

Teaching us that, denying ungodliness and worldly lusts, we should live soberly, righteously, and godly, in this present world.

Titus 2:12

Let us walk honestly, as in the day; not in rioting and drunkenness, not in chambering and wantonness, not in strife and envying.

But put ye on the Lord Jesus Christ, and make not provision for the flesh, to fulfil the lusts thereof.

Romans 13:13-14

. . .be grave, not doubletongued, not given to much wine, not greedy of filthy lucre.

1 Timothy 3:8 (partial)

Therefore let us not sleep, as do others; but let us watch and be sober.

For they that sleep sleep in the night; and they that be drunken are drunken in the night.

1 Thessalonians 5:6-7

But I keep under my body, and bring it into subjection: lest that by any means, when I have preached to others, I myself should be a castaway.

1 Corinthians 9:27

. . .neither fornicators, nor idolaters, nor adulterers, nor effeminate, nor abusers of themselves with mankind,

Nor thieves, nor covetous, nor drunkards, nor revilers, nor extortioners, shall inherit the kingdom of God.

And such were some of you: but ye are washed, but ye are sanctified, but ye are justified in the name of the Lord Jesus, and by the Spirit of our God.

1 Corinthians 6:9(partial)-11

SELFLESS

And if thy hand offend thee, cut it off: it is better for thee to enter into life maimed, than having two hands to go into hell, into the fire that never shall be quenched.

Mark 9:43

But God forbid that I should glory, save in the cross of our Lord Jesus Christ, by whom the world is crucified unto me, and I unto the world.

Galatians 6:14

And he said unto them, Verily I say unto you, There is no man that hath left house, or parents, or brethren, or wife, or children, for the kingdom of God's sake,

Who shall not receive manifold more in this present time, and in the world to come life everlasting.

Luke 18:29-30

Again, the kingdom of heaven is like unto a merchant man, seeking goodly pearls:

Who, when he had found one pearl of great price, went and sold all that he had, and bought it.

Matthew 13:45-46

Blessed is the man that endureth temptation: for when he is tried, he shall receive the crown of life, which the Lord hath promised to them that love him.

James 1:12

We then that are strong ought to bear the infirmities of the weak, and not to please ourselves.

Romans 15:1

If others be partakers of this power over you, are not we rather? Nevertheless we have not used this power; but suffer all things, lest we should hinder the gospel of Christ.

1 Corinthians 9:12

And he said to them all, If any man will come after me, let him deny himself, and take up his cross daily, and follow me.

For whosoever will save his life shall lose it: but whosoever will lose his life for my sake, the same shall save it.

Luke 9:23-24

He that loveth his life shall lose it; and he that hateth his life in this world shall keep it unto life eternal.

John 12:25

I am crucified with Christ: nevertheless I live; yet not I, but Christ liveth in me: and the life which I now live in the flesh I live by the faith of the Son of God, who loved me, and gave himself for me.

Galatians 2:20

And whosoever doth not bear his cross, and come after me, cannot be my disciple.

Luke 14:27

But what things were gain to me, those I counted loss for Christ.

Yea doubtless, and I count all things but loss for the excellency of the knowledge of Christ Jesus my Lord: for whom I have suffered the loss of all things, and do count them but dung, that I may win Christ.

Philippians 3:7-8

Forasmuch then as Christ hath suffered for us in the flesh, arm yourselves likewise with the same mind: for he that hath suffered in the flesh hath ceased from sin;

That he no longer should live the rest of his time in the flesh to the lusts of men, but to the will of God.

1 Peter 4:1-2

And a certain scribe came, and said unto him, Master, I will follow thee whithersoever thou goest.

And Jesus saith unto him, The foxes have holes, and the birds of the air have nests; but the Son of man hath not where to lay his head.

Matthew 8:19-20

This I say then, Walk in the Spirit, and ye shall not fulfil the lust of the flesh.

For the flesh lusteth against the Spirit, and the Spirit against the flesh: and these are contrary the one to the other: so that ye cannot do the things that ye would.

Galatians 5:16-17

No man that warreth entangleth himself with the affairs of this life; that he may please him who hath chosen him to be a soldier.

2 Timothy 2:4

SINCERE

That ye may approve things that are excellent; that ye may be sincere and without offence till the day of Christ.

Philippians 1:10

Blessed is the man unto whom the LORD imputeth not iniquity, and in whose spirit there is no guile.

Psalm 32:2

But let us, who are of the day, be sober, putting on the breastplate of faith and love; and for an helmet, the hope of salvation.

1 Thessalonians 5:8

For we are not as many, which corrupt the word of God: but as of sincerity, but as of God, in the sight of God speak we in Christ.

2 Corinthians 2:17

Now the end of the commandment is charity out of a pure heart, and of a good conscience, and of faith unfeigned.

1 Timothy 1:5

For our rejoicing is this, the testimony of our conscience, that in simplicity and godly sincerity, not with fleshly wisdom, but by the grace of God, we have had our conversation in the world, and more abundantly to you-ward.

2 Corinthians 1:12

For our exhortation was not of deceit, nor of uncleanness, nor in guile:

But as we were allowed of God to be put in trust with the gospel, even so we speak; not as pleasing men, but God, which trieth our hearts.

For neither at any time used we flattering words, as ye know, nor a cloke of covetousness; God is witness.

1 Thessalonians 2:3-5

As newborn babes, desire the sincere milk of the word, that ye may grow thereby.

1 Peter 2:2

Now therefore fear the LORD, and serve him in sincerity and in truth. . . .

Joshua 24:14 (partial)

Grace be with all them that love our Lord Jesus Christ in sincerity. Amen.

Ephesians 6:24

Let love be without dissimulation. Abhor that which is evil; cleave to that which is good.

Romans 12:9

Seeing ye have purified your souls in obeying the truth through the Spirit unto unfeigned love of the brethren, see that ye love one another with a pure heart fervently:

1 Peter 1:22

Therefore let us keep the feast, not with old leaven, neither with the leaven of malice and wickedness; but with the unleavened bread of sincerity and truth.

1 Corinthians 5:8

Wherefore gird up the loins of your mind, be sober, and hope to the end for the grace that is to be brought unto you at the revelation of Jesus Christ.

1 Peter 1:13

For I say, through the grace given unto me, to every man that is among you, not to think of himself more highly than he ought to think; but to think soberly, according as God hath dealt to every man the measure of faith.

Romans 12:3

Wherefore laying aside all malice, and all guile, and hypocrisies, and envies, and all evil speakings.

1 Peter 2:1

What will ye do in the solemn day, and in the day of the feast of the LORD?

Hosea 9:5

I speak not by commandment, but by occasion of the forwardness of others, and to prove the sincerity of your love.

2 Corinthians 8:8

Young men likewise exhort to be sober minded.

Titus 2:6

And in their mouth was found no guile: for they are without fault before the throne of God.

Revelations 14:5

SOBER (NOT DRUNKEN)

. . .drunkenness, revellings, and such like: of the which I tell you before, as I have also told you in time past, that they which do such things shall not inherit the kingdom of God.

Galatians 5:21 (partial)

Who hath woe? who hath sorrow? who hath contentions? who hath babbling? who hath wounds without cause? who hath redness of eyes?

They that tarry long at the wine; they that go to seek mixed wine.

Look not thou upon the wine when it is red, when it giveth his colour in the cup, when it moveth itself aright.

At the last it biteth like a serpent, and stingeth like an adder.

Proverbs 23:29-32

Now therefore beware, I pray thee, and drink not wine nor strong drink, and eat not any unclean thing.

Judges 13:4

For he shall be great in the sight of the Lord, and shall drink neither wine nor strong drink; and he shall be filled with the Holy Ghost, even from his mother's womb.

Luke 1:15

Woe unto him that giveth his neighbour drink, that puttest thy bottle to him, and makest him drunken also, that thou mayest look on their nakedness!

Habakkuk 2:15

Wine is a mocker, strong drink is raging: and whosoever is deceived thereby is not wise.

Proverbs 20:1

Whoredom and wine and new wine take away the heart.

Hosea 4:11

For while they be folden together as thorns, and while they are drunken as drunkards, they shall be devoured as stubble fully dry.

Nahum 1:10

Woe unto them that rise up early in the morning, that they may follow strong drink; that continue until night, till wine inflame them!

Isaiah 5:11

And take heed to yourselves, lest at any time your hearts be overcharged with surfeiting, and drunkenness, and cares of this life, and so that day come upon you unawares.

Luke 21:34

And they have cast lots for my people; and
have given a boy for an harlot, and sold a
girl for wine, that they might drink.

Joel 3:3

For the drunkard and the glutton shall
come to poverty: and drowsiness shall
clothe a man with rags.

Proverbs 23:21

TACTFUL

The heart of the wise teacheth his mouth,
and addeth learning to his lips.
Pleasant words are as an honeycomb,
sweet to the soul, and health to the bones.

Proverbs 16:23-24

A fool uttereth all his mind: but a wise
man keepeth it in till afterwards.

Proverbs 29:11

In the multitude of words there wanteth
not sin: but he that refraineth his lips is
wise.

Proverbs 10:19

For though I would desire to glory, I shall
not be a fool; for I will say the truth: but
now I forbear, lest any man should think of
me above that which he seeth me to be, or
that he heareth of me.

2 Corinthians 12:6

A word fitly spoken is like apples of gold in pictures of silver.

Proverbs 25:11

And unto the Jews I became as a Jew, that I might gain the Jews; to them that are under the law, as under the law, that I might gain them that are under the law;

To them that are without law, as without law, (being not without law to God, but under the law to Christ,) that I might gain them that are without law.

1 Corinthians 9:20-21

Let your speech be alway with grace, seasoned with salt, that ye may know how ye ought to answer every man.

Colossians 4:6

The heart of the righteous studieth to answer: but the mouth of the wicked poureth out evil things.

Proverbs 15:28

There is that speaketh like the piercings of a sword: but the tongue of the wise is health.

Proverbs 12:18

. . .If any man offend not in word, the same is a perfect man, and able also to bridle the whole body.

James 3:2 (partial)

A man hath joy by the answer of his mouth: and a word spoken in due season, how good is it!

Proverbs 15:23

A talebearer revealeth secrets: but he that is of a faithful spirit concealeth the matter.

Proverbs 11:13

A time to rend, and a time to sew; a time to keep silence, and a time to speak.

Ecclesiastes 3:7

Set a watch, O LORD, before my mouth; keep the door of my lips.

Psalm 141:3

THANKFUL

And he took the seven loaves and the fishes, and gave thanks, and brake them, and gave to his disciples, and the disciples to the multitude.

Matthew 15:36

Giving thanks always for all things unto God and the Father in the name of our Lord Jesus Christ.

Ephesians 5:20

In every thing give thanks: for this is the will of God in Christ Jesus concerning you.

1 Thessalonians 5:18

I will praise thee, O LORD, with my whole heart; I will shew forth all thy marvellous works.

I will be glad and rejoice in thee: I will sing praise to thy name, O thou most High.

Psalm 9:1-2

And they, continuing daily with one accord in the temple, and breaking bread from house to house, did eat their meat with gladness and singleness of heart,

Praising God, and having favour with all the people. And the Lord added to the church daily such as should be saved.

Acts 2:46-47

That I may publish with the voice of thanksgiving, and tell of all thy wondrous works.

Psalm 26:7

Blessed be the LORD, that hath given rest unto his people Israel, according to all that he promised: there hath not failed one word of all his good promise, which he promised by the hand of Moses his servant.

1 Kings 8:56

Blessed be the Lord, who daily loadeth us with benefits, even the God of our salvation. Selah.

Psalm 68:19

And he took the cup, and gave thanks, and gave it to them, saying, Drink ye all of it.

Matthew 26:27

O LORD, thou hast brought up my soul from the grave: thou hast kept me alive, that I should not go down to the pit.

Psalm 30:3

I will mention the lovingkindnesss of the LORD, and the praises of the LORD, according to all that the LORD hath bestowed on us, and the great goodness toward the house of Israel, which he hath bestowed on them according to his mercies, and according to the multitude of his lovingkindnesses.

Isaiah 63:7

Thou hast turned for me my mourning into dancing: thou hast put off my sackcloth, and girded me with gladness;

To the end that my glory may sing praise to thee, and not be silent. O LORD my God, I will give thanks unto thee for ever.

Psalm 30:11-12

O give thanks unto the LORD; for he is good: for his mercy endureth for ever.

Psalm 136:1

I thank thee, and praise thee, O thou God of my fathers, who hast given me wisdom and might, and hast made known unto me now what we desired of thee: for thou hast now made known unto us the king's matter.

Daniel 2:23

Many, O LORD my God, are thy wonderful works which thou hast done, and thy thoughts which are to us-ward: they cannot be reckoned up in order unto thee: if I would declare and speak of them, they are more than can be numbered.

Psalm 40:5

He that regardeth the day, regardeth it unto the Lord; and he that regardeth not the day, to the Lord he doth not regard it. He that eateth, eateth to the Lord, for he giveth God thanks; and he that eateth not, to the Lord he eateth not, and giveth God thanks.

Romans 14:6

It is a good thing to give thanks unto the LORD, and to sing praises unto thy name, O most High:

To shew forth thy lovingkindness in the morning, and thy faithfulness every night.

Psalm 92:1-2

UNDERSTANDING

If there be therefore any consolation in Christ, if any comfort of love, if any fellowship of the Spirit, if any bowels and mercies,

Fulfil ye my joy, that ye be likeminded, having the same love, being of one accord, of one mind.

Philippians 2:1-2

But let him that glorieth glory in this, that he understandeth and knoweth me, that I am the LORD which exercise lovingkindness, judgment, and righteousness, in the earth: for in these things I delight, saith the LORD.

Jeremiah 9:24

Then shalt thou understand the fear of the LORD, and find the knowledge of God.

For the LORD giveth wisdom: out of his mouth cometh knowledge and understanding.

Proverbs 2:5-6

When I was a child, I spake as a child, I understood as a child, I thought as a child: but when I became a man, I put away childish things.

1 Corinthians 13:11

Evil men understand not judgment: but they that seek the LORD understand all things.

Proverbs 28:5

The tongue of the wise useth knowledge aright: but the mouth of fools poureth out foolishness.

Proverbs 15:2

Justice and judgment are the habitation of thy throne: mercy and truth shall go before thy face.

Psalm 89:14

And unto man he said, Behold, the fear of the Lord, that is wisdom; and to depart from evil is understanding.

Job 28:28

In the lips of him that hath understanding wisdom is found: but a rod is for the back of him that is void of understanding.

Proverbs 10:13

But thou, O Lord, art a God full of compassion, and gracious, longsuffering, and plenteous in mercy and truth.

Psalm 86:15

With the ancient is wisdom; and in length of days understanding.

With him is wisdom and strength, he hath counsel and understanding.

Job 12:12-13

Wisdom resteth in the heart of him that hath understanding: but that which is in the midst of fools is made known.

Proverbs 14:33

Make me to understand the way of thy precepts: so shall I talk of thy wondrous works.

Psalm 119:27

VIGILANT

Be sober, be vigilant; because your adversary the devil, as a roaring lion, walketh about, seeking whom he may devour.

1 Peter 5:8

Watch and pray, that ye enter not into temptation: the spirit indeed is willing, but the flesh is weak.

Matthew 26:41

Let thine eyes look right on, and let thine eyelids look straight before thee.

Ponder the path of thy feet, and let all thy ways be established.

Proverbs 4:25-26

He that dasheth in pieces is come up before thy face: keep the munition, watch the way, make thy loins strong, fortify thy power mightily.

Nahum 2:1

But watch thou in all things, endure afflictions, do the work of an evangelist, make full proof of thy ministry.

2 Timothy 4:5

I will stand upon my watch, and set me upon the tower, and will watch to see what he will say unto me, and what I shall answer when I am reproved.

Habakkuk 2:1

Watch ye therefore, and pray always, that ye may be accounted worthy to escape all these things that shall come to pass, and to stand before the Son of man.

Luke 21:36

I watch, and am as a sparrow alone upon the house top.

Psalm 102:7

Blessed is the man that heareth me, watching daily at my gates, waiting at the posts of my doors.

Proverbs 8:34

Watch therefore: for ye know not what hour your Lord doth come.

But know this, that if the goodman of the house had known in what watch the thief would come, he would have watched, and would not have suffered his house to be broken up.

Matthew 24:42-43

Look to yourselves, that we lose not those things which we have wrought, but that we receive a full reward.

2 John 8

And then if any man shall say to you, Lo, here is Christ; or, lo, he is there; believe him not:

For false Christs and false prophets shall rise, and shall shew signs and wonders, to seduce, if it were possible, even the elect.

But take ye heed: behold, I have foretold you all things.

Mark 13:21-23

And what I say unto you I say unto all, Watch.

Mark 13:37

WISE

Therefore whosoever heareth these sayings of mine, and doeth them, I will liken him unto a wise man, which built his house upon a rock:

And the rain descended, and the floods came, and the winds blew, and beat upon that house; and it fell not: for it was founded upon a rock.

Matthew 7:24-25

My son, attend to my words; incline thine ear unto my sayings.

Let them not depart from thine eyes; keep them in the midst of thine heart.

For they are life unto those that find them, and health to all their flesh.

Proverbs 4:20-22

With him is strength and wisdom: the deceived and the deceiver are his.

He leadeth counsellors away spoiled, and maketh the judges fools.

Job 12:16-17

The LORD by wisdom hath founded the earth; by understanding hath he established the heavens.

By his knowledge the depths are broken up, and the clouds drop down the dew.

My son, let not them depart from thine eyes: keep sound wisdom and discretion.

Proverbs 3:19-21

He that is void of wisdom despiseth his neighbour: but a man of understanding holdeth his peace.

Proverbs 11:12

Let the word of Christ dwell in you richly in all wisdom; teaching and admonishing one another in psalms and hymns and spiritual songs, singing with grace in your hearts to the Lord.

Colossians 3:16

Be wise now therefore, O ye kings: be instructed, ye judges of the earth.

Psalm 2:10

Wherefore be ye not unwise, but understanding what the will of the Lord is.

Ephesians 5:17

My son, eat thou honey, because it is good; and the honeycomb, which is sweet to thy taste:

So shall the knowledge of wisdom be unto thy soul: when thou hast found it, then there shall be a reward, and thy expectation shall not be cut off.

Proverbs 24:13-14

Whoso is wise, and will observe these things, even they shall understand the lovingkindness of the LORD.

Psalm 107:43

For your obedience is come abroad unto all men. I am glad therefore on your behalf: but yet I would have you wise unto that which is good, and simple concerning evil.

Romans 16:19

Say unto wisdom, Thou art my sister; and call understanding thy kinswoman:

Proverbs 7:4

The law of the wise is a fountain of life, to depart from the snares of death.

Good understanding giveth favour: but the way of transgressors is hard.

Proverbs 13:14-15

How much better is it to get wisdom than gold! and to get understanding rather to be chosen than silver!

Proverbs 16:16

And wisdom and knowledge shall be the stability of thy times, and strength of salvation: the fear of the LORD is his treasure.

Isaiah 33:6

Howbeit we speak wisdom among them that are perfect: yet not the wisdom of this world, nor of the princes of this world, that come to nought:

But we speak the wisdom of God in a mystery, even the hidden wisdom, which God ordained before the world unto our glory:

Which none of the princes of this world knew: for had they known it, they would not have crucified the Lord of glory.

1 Corinthians 2:6-8